RENEWED AND TRANSFORMED

A STUDY IN WHAT IT MEANS TO LIVE WITH THE MIND OF CHRIST

ALYSSA J HOWARD

Unless otherwise indicated, all Scripture quotations taken from the New American Standard Bible® (NASB), Copyright © 1960, 1962, 1963, 1968, 1971, 1972, 1973, 1975, 1977, 1995 by The Lockman Foundation. Used by permission. www.Lockman.org

ISBN-10: 1985309130
ISBN-13: 978-1985309135

CONTENTS

Introduction

BE TRANSFORMED

And do not be conformed to this world, but be transformed by the renewing of your mind, so that you may prove what the will of God is, that which is good and acceptable and perfect. **– Romans 12:2**

I've heard this verse many times throughout my years as a Christian. But what does it mean to renew your mind? My hope is that throughout the next eight weeks you will join me in discovering just what it means to live your life with the mind of Christ. But before we dive into the study, let's take a look at three popular definitions of renewing your mind and why they might be a bit misleading.

- **In order to renew your mind, you have to change your behavior.**

It's pretty easy to see how we arrived at this definition. The verse tells us to "not be conformed to this world." So obviously, there must be some element of behavior involved in renewing your mind. The problem, however, lies in the fact that true behavior change follows internal transformation... not the other way around. You can try to change your behavior for a time with moderate success, but true change happens when we are <u>transformed</u> from the inside out. So if you believe you have to renew your mind every day by behaving like a Christian rather than conforming to this world, you will most likely miss the most crucial element of mind renewal... being *transformed*.

- **Renewing your mind is all up to you.**

Again, there is some truth to this definition. You certainly play an active role in renewing your mind daily. But by making it all up to you, you are once again missing a key piece to the puzzle… transformation by the power of the Holy Spirit. The truth is that if it were possible to renew your mind apart from Him, the Law would have been enough to cause the nation of Israel to renew their minds. We know, however, that it wasn't enough. No matter how much effort they put forth, they couldn't change their thinking to align with Christ's. We also know that the world tries to renew their minds this way. They accomplish this through positive thinking, motivational speeches, and self-help teachings. But without the Holy Spirit, these methods will only take them so far.

- **Renewing your mind is all about reading and memorizing Scripture.**

I see this definition more often than the others. While the Bible plays a key role in teaching us how to think, Scripture alone isn't enough. Yes, you read that right. The truth is that the Bible is alive and active <u>only</u> by the power of the Holy Spirit. Without Him, it's simply a book with words. He is the one who breathes life into the pages, and He is the one working in your heart and life when you read. You can study and memorize Scripture all you want, but unless you allow the Holy Spirit to work in your heart and allow Him to transform your thinking, you will not be renewing your mind.

In the end, renewing your mind is about being transformed.

The Bible is certainly an imperative tool in learning how to think like Christ, and you do play an active role in changing your thinking as well. But apart from the transforming power of the Holy Spirit, your efforts won't amount to much.

I pray that as you work through this study that you would allow Him to move in your heart and mind. Allow Him to transform your thinking in a way you never thought possible.

Week 1: Defining What It Means to Renew Your Mind

THE IMPORTANCE OF RENEWING YOUR MIND

Up until recently, I wasn't sure what renewing your mind actually looked like in practice. I knew I was supposed to do it, and I was aware that it was a daily process. But I wasn't certain about the practicality behind it. *What does a "renewed mind" look like? Is it something God does for me? Or do I have a role to play?*

The more I dove into the Scriptures, the more I realized that that Bible had quite a bit to say about our thought life. In fact, I began to learn how crucial our thought life is to our faith. We cannot be productive for the Kingdom, love the way we're called to love, or even experience God's peace and joy without first renewing our minds. *It's <u>that</u> important.*

Renewing your mind is an integral part of your Christian walk – one that you have to be diligent about on a daily basis.

4 BIBLICAL BENEFITS OF A RENEWED MIND

The Bible tells us to be "transformed by the renewing of our minds." But what does it really mean to have a renewed mind? As followers of Christ, we aren't just called to live differently, but we are called to think differently as well.

Changing the way we think may seem like a daunting task. It certainly requires a bit of discipline. If I'm going to change the way I think, I have to be diligent and aware of what I'm thinking about and make changes when necessary. I have to make choices about what I allow my mind to dwell on. **We may not have control over the thoughts that spontaneously enter our minds, but we certainly have control over the thoughts we allow to stay.**

So why go through all of this trouble in the first place? Is having a renewed mind worth it?

- **We learn to discern the will of God. (Romans 12:2)**

- **We grow closer to God and become more like Him in the process. (Colossians 3:10)**

- **A renewed mind helps us to recognize our true identities in Christ. (Colossians 3:1-3)**

- **We find life and peace beyond understanding when we allow our minds to be transformed by the Holy Spirit. (Romans 8:5-6)**

These are just four of the benefits associated with having a renewed mind in Christ. There are certainly countless more. We more readily love and forgive others. We develop a hatred towards sin and worldly living. Abiding in Him becomes second nature, and we daily experience the fruit of the Spirit in our lives. *I don't know about you, but I'd say these are some pretty amazing benefits!*

When we daily renew our minds, we begin to see the world through the eyes of our Savior.

So what does it really mean to be transformed by the renewing of our minds? The word "transformed" should serve as a clue.

Renewing the mind results in complete transformation. No longer a slave to the power of sin. No longer living a life that leads to death. But rather we are transformed into a new creation - a child of God.

SO WHERE DO I BEGIN?

We know that renewing your mind is important, and we've studied the benefits. But where do we begin exactly? If renewing your mind is a process, what does that process entail? Fortunately, the Bible gives us quite a bit of insight into where to start.

Seven practical steps to begin renewing your mind:

- **Pray.**

Pray without ceasing. This is most definitely the key to daily renewing your mind. God is on our side, and He desires for us to grow and mature in Him. Pray and ask Him to help you as you endeavor to change your thinking.

- **Understand where worldly thinking originates.**

The enemy hates it when we change our thinking, and he will do anything he can to keep us from doing so. He will plant seeds of doubt, temptations, worry, defeat, low self-worth… you name it and he will try it.

- **Be prepared to combat lies with the truth.**

Do you know your Bible? The enemy certainly does. He knows the truth and hates hearing it. Since we know that worldly thinking comes from him, we can combat his lies with the truth of God's Word. So make sure you know it!

- **Do what is necessary to guard and protect your mind.**

This seems to be the step that trips us up the most, myself included. There are many ways to guard our minds against worldly thinking. One way is by combatting the enemy's lies with the truth (as we already pointed out). Another way, however, is to make sure that what we put into our minds is worthy of Christ. When it comes to movies, music, and other forms of entertainment, are we putting things in our minds that should be there?

- **Take every thought captive and make them obedient to Christ.**

Thoughts are going to enter our minds. There's no doubt about that. But we do have the authority to take our thoughts captive. Allowing them to stay and take root is up to us. (And trust me when I say that it's much easier to remove a thought *before* it takes root rather than after!)

- **Make the conscious choice to think about the right things.**

The Bible doesn't just say to stop thinking like the world; rather it tells us to start thinking like Christ. Renewing your mind involves replacing worldly thoughts with godly ones. *How much time do we devote to thinking about the things of God?*

- **Repeat these steps daily (hourly if needed.)**

All of these steps are meant to be repeated. It's certainly a process – one that grows easier each and every day. We simply need to be diligent, keep at it, and allow the Holy Spirit to transform our thinking.

Trust me when I say that it will be worth it.

Week 1 Study Guide:

- What role does the mind play in your daily Christian walk? How does it shape your faith?

- Read Ephesians 4:21-24. What do we learn about the process of renewing your mind from this passage? What role does the Holy Spirit play? What role do you play as a believer?

- Read Romans 12:2 and Colossians 3:10. What promises do we receive when we choose to renew our minds in Christ?

- Read Colossians 3:1-3. What does the Bible say about you now that you are a child of God? What role does our mind play in that new identity?

- In this lesson, we learned about some amazing benefits to renewing your mind. Can you think of any other reasons why we should make renewing our minds a priority?

- Of the seven steps to renewing your mind, which one do you think is the most important and why?

- Which one of the steps do you believe to be most difficult to put into practice? Why do you think that is?

- Read 2 Corinthians 10:5. What does it mean to "take your thoughts captive"?

Week 2: The Art of Changing Your Mind

SIN NATURE VS THE HOLY SPIRIT: WHO'S IN CONTROL?

Have you ever given any thought to who or what controls your thought life? Up until recently, I considered my thoughts to be my own. I understood that the enemy sometimes plants doubts or temptations. I also knew that I was supposed to think about the things of God, seeking first His Kingdom. But I never really thought about the concept of control. And no, I'm not talking about "mind control." Rather I'm talking about the kind of control a driver has over his vehicle.

Who is really at the wheel of my thought life?

Let's break this down…

For most of my Christian life, I believed that my sinful nature and my new God-given nature were at war with each other. In my eyes, they were equal adversaries creating a conflict within me. And while it's true that these two natures contradict one another, I'm not sure that "equal adversaries" is the best way to describe them.

Therefore there is now no condemnation for those who are in Christ Jesus. For the law of the Spirit of life in Christ Jesus has set you free from the law of sin and of death. – Romans 8:1-2

As I pondered these verses, I couldn't help but ask myself one question. Who is more powerful – the Holy Spirit or my old sinful nature?

If you have the Holy Spirit, then you have a power within you that is far greater than your old, sinful nature.

The power of sin is no match for the Holy Spirit.

Now those who belong to Christ Jesus have crucified the flesh with its passions and desires. If we live by the Spirit, let us also walk by the Spirit. – Galatians 5:24-25

The flesh has been crucified. It holds no power in our lives any longer. But it is up to us to "keep in step" with the Spirit. We have to abide in Christ.

Before Christ, we had no choice – our sinful nature was in control of our thought life. *But in Christ, we do have a choice.* We can give the Holy Spirit control. And when He is in control, the sinful nature has to take a backseat. He doesn't get to drive.

So is it possible for our sinful nature to take control and drive our thoughts? Yes, but only if we give him the keys. And I don't know about you, but I never want to give him the keys again!

In the words of Paul, "Since we have died to sin, how can we continue to live in it?" (Romans 6:2) Let's choose instead to live by the Spirit.

So who's in control of your thoughts? Do we make the conscious choice to give the Holy Spirit control? Or do we allow our sinful natures to take the wheel?

WHY TRUE REPENTENCE REQUIRES A CHANGE OF MIND

Christians hear the word *repentance* quite often. It's an essential part of our faith, to say the least. As a child, I was taught that it meant being sorry for your sins. But as I grew older, I began to see that true repentance extends far beyond a simple, "I'm sorry." Rather, it's a complete transformation.

The Greek word most commonly translated as "repent" in the New Testament is *metanoeo* (or *metanoia* in its noun form). It means "to change one's mind or purpose."

So when Jesus told us to repent, He wasn't simply telling us to be sorry for our sins. Rather, He was asking us to change our minds – to turn our thoughts away from sin and towards God instead.

Jesus clearly demonstrated this in the gospel of Mark when He said:

... *"The time is fulfilled, and the kingdom of God is at hand; repent and believe in the gospel." – Mark 1:15*

Jesus wasn't simply asking them to say sorry. He made it clear that entering the Kingdom of God is a two-step process - turning our minds away from sin and setting our sights on Him.

It's not enough to be sorry – true repentance requires a complete change of mind.

Up until the time of Christ, the Law of Moses gave clear instructions on how to act and behave as God's people. It was mostly about a person's actions, at least that's how the religious teachers perceived it. They would regularly boast about their "righteous deeds." In fact, they even added laws to make themselves feel more righteous.

But Jesus changed the game...

The Pharisees believed they were righteous because of their actions. Jesus turned things upside down when He stated that true righteousness stems from a heart that longs to please God.

We should be more focused on our minds than our actions. Why? Because when our heart and minds are in line, our actions follow. And not only do our actions follow, but they stem from an obedient heart with good intentions. The Pharisees had their virtuous deeds, but they weren't following God with their hearts. Their actions stemmed from pride and the need to look good in front of others.

So will you join me in thinking consciously about what it means to change your mind?

True repentance isn't just about turning away from sinful <u>actions</u>; rather we have to make the choice to change our minds and turn away from sinful <u>thinking</u>.

And as we turn our minds away from sin, we replace those thoughts with our hope in Jesus Christ, and we allow the Holy Spirit to transform us from the inside out.

Does renewing your mind ever seem like an impossible task? For me personally, changing the way my mind thinks and processes information seems like an intimidating task. But there is hope! (Thank goodness - right?) When the Bible discusses the idea of renewing your mind, it places most of the emphasis on us. We have to be the ones to make the choice to think differently, but that doesn't mean God left us empty-handed. In fact, He never calls us to do something He hasn't already equipped us to do.

Imagine you are wearing a tool belt...

Here are three tools you will find in that belt to help you in your task of renewing your mind:

- **The Bible**

This is single-handedly one of the most amazing tools we have as believers in teaching us the truth about who God is, what He has done for us, and how we should live as His children.

When it comes to renewing our minds, the Bible gives us the knowledge we need to combat the lies of this world. After all, Jesus responded with Scripture when the enemy tested Him in the wilderness. Because it is "God-breathed," we can trust it as a source of truth and we can rely on it when we are faced with doubts or challenging times.

I also can't emphasize enough how important it is to know God's Word and to know it well. It's not enough to simply read a little bit here and there, it needs to be in us. We need to hide His Word in our hearts. We need to be ready to combat the lies of the enemy when he tries to plant seeds of doubt in our minds.

If we fill our minds with the truth, there will be no room left for the enemy's lies.

- **Our Brothers and Sisters in Christ**

Looking back throughout His Word, it's pretty clear that God is all about relationships. He cares about how we love each other. If you look at the Ten Commandments, for example, you'll notice that six of the ten are about how we relate to one another. The Law taught the Jewish people to love each other as they loved themselves. *But Jesus took love to another level....*

We aren't just called to love others as we love ourselves, but rather we are called to love the same way Jesus loved us – *sacrificially and unconditionally.* He forgave us even before we repented of our sins.

Jesus left to prepare a place for us; and while He is away, one of the most amazing gifts He gave to us was each other. When we are born again into the family of God, we literally inherit a family of believers to lean on. And at the same time, we need to be readily available to be leaned on by our brothers and sisters in the faith.

It's also important that we strive to live at peace with one another. Paul talks about unity in faith countless times throughout the New Testament. We can't be at odds with one another and expect to grow as the body of Christ. Disunity weakens the body, while unforgiveness and bitterness weaken us individually.

When it comes to the mind, bitterness and offense always get in the way of spiritual growth.

- **The Holy Spirit**

I saved this one for last because I believe it to be the most important. It's the Holy Spirit who transforms our hearts and minds. He is responsible for teaching us how to live righteously. He gives us boldness to share Christ, and He comforts us through difficult times.

Without the Holy Spirit, the other two tools on this list don't mean as much. It's the Holy Spirit that illuminates God's Word and makes it alive and active. And it's by the Holy Spirit that we can identify ourselves as children of God and love one another unconditionally as Christ loved us.

Are we allowing the Holy Spirit to do His job? In order to grow, we have to give Him control. He needs to take the wheel and lead us where He wants us to go. It's impossible to grow spiritually by our own doing; true spiritual growth only occurs by the power of the Holy Spirit.

I'll be honest… it's easy to say things like "give the Holy Spirit control." But in practice, giving Him complete control can be hard. We have to continually make the choice to keep Him in the driver's seat – to keep the faith even when things grow difficult.

I think of Peter who stepped out in faith and walked on water with Jesus. He not only had to be brave enough to step out of the boat, but he had to maintain his faith even when everything around him said, "You're going to sink."

The best part of that story, however, is that even though he made the mistake of taking his eyes off of Jesus for a moment, Jesus was still faithful. Even when we feel weak, if we surrender our weakness to God, He is faithful to pick us up. He gives us the strength we need to endure anything that comes our way, and He will remind us as many times as it takes to keep our focus on Him.

The Holy Spirit reminds us of our hope in Jesus when the world around us seems utterly hopeless.

With the help of the Holy Spirit, God's Word, and our family in Christ, there is hope when it comes to changing your thought life. God certainly equipped us with everything we need to live in Him with a renewed mind.

Week 2 Study Guide:

- Read Romans 8:5-9. As a child of God, who or what controls you? What does this passage say about the sin nature?

- Read Romans 6:6-7. What does the Bible say happened to your sin nature? In light of this truth, why do you suppose we still struggle with sin?

- Read Matthew 5:21-22, 27-28. How did Jesus' teaching about sin challenge the people of His day, especially the Pharisees?

- In your own words, define what it means to live in a state of repentance.

- Read 2 Timothy 3:14-17. How did Paul define the Scriptures and its purpose in our lives?

- Read 1 Corinthians 2:14-16. What role does the Holy Spirit play in our thinking? What's the difference between someone who has the mind of Christ verses someone who does not?

- In 1 Corinthians 3:1-4, Paul told the people of Corinth that they were still like "infants" in the faith and that they were allowing themselves to be controlled by their sinful natures. But just a few verses earlier, he told them that they possessed the mind of Christ. What does this tell you about the mind of Christ? (Hint: Is it possible to have it and not be using it?)

- In this unit, we discussed three amazing tools that God had given us to help us renew our minds. Since the enemy's main goal is to keep us from growing spiritually, what are some practical ways that He might try to keep us from putting these tools to use? How can we combat His tactics?

Week 3: Worldly Thinking vs Godly Thinking

IS IT BIBLICAL TO HAVE AN OPEN MIND?

Is it biblical to have an open mind? Many in the church today would probably say no. Open-mindedness is often associated with worldly thinking and culture. It's an acceptance of all faiths and lifestyles in a way that says, "There are many paths to God." But the truth is that open-mindedness was actually God's idea. Not in the way that it's preached today, but in a way that says, "My mind is open to things of God, and I want to fill it with nothing but Him."

But don't take my word for it. Here's what the Bible has to say about it:

Now He said to them, "These are My words which I spoke to you while I was still with you, that all things which are written about Me in the Law of Moses and the Prophets and the Psalms must be fulfilled." Then He opened their minds to understand the Scriptures. - Luke 24:44-45

And here's what the Bible has to say about having a mind that is closed:

They do not know, nor do they understand, for He has smeared over their eyes so that they cannot see and their hearts so that they cannot comprehend. - Isaiah 44:18

I couldn't help but notice one important thing as I read these passages. - an open mind leads to understanding and salvation, but a closed mind makes us blind to the truth.

The enemy has no ability to create, so he makes every effort to distort, mimic, and/or redefine the things of God. **The enemy's definition of having an open mind is tolerance.** We open our minds and fill it with anything and everything. But that was never God's intention. *He longed for our minds to be open so that we could fill it with nothing but Him.*

So how do we pursue an open mind in Christ?

When we turn to Jesus, we are given an "open" mind. In other words, the veil of our mind is removed, and we can clearly see the truth.

Apart from Jesus, our minds are closed off. The truth of God's Word sounds like foolishness, and we lack understanding when it comes to things of God.

So the choice is ultimately ours to make, do we turn to Christ with our hearts and minds open? Or do we choose to live behind a veil in darkness?

POSITIVE THINKING WAS GOD'S DESIGN

The world knows that positive thinking is good for us. Nearly every self-help book on the market will tell you that your mind plays a crucial role in shaping not only your life but also your health.

I used to believe that positive thinking belonged to the world. I would see "positive" encouragements online (with the absence of God of course) and think to myself how wrong the whole positive thinking movement was. The problem with that, however, is that positive thinking was God's idea first. The world simply took a spiritual truth, removed God, and packaged it up for everyone who needed it.

It caught on because it works. And it works, because it's a God-given spiritual truth.

Speaking from experience, it's not easy to keep my mind positive all day, every day. In fact, it's downright hard sometimes – especially during difficult circumstances. But I truly believe that God's desire for our minds is that we learn to replace our negative thoughts with positive thoughts - *that we fill our mind with His truth, His love, and His peace.*

The world may have caught on that positive thinking is good for us, but they are missing a key element to finding true happiness and success – our Savior Jesus Christ.

We can tell the world to choose joy or to rejoice in hard times, but God gave us something to always be joyful about. So even when times are tough, we still have Jesus. We still have the love of God and His salvation. And we can hold on to the hope of a future with Him.

And what of peace? Is it possible to have peace during difficult times apart from Christ? The Bible tells that the peace of Christ "transcends all understanding." In other words, when the world would find it impossible to experience peace of mind, we can have peace in Jesus.

So how do we experience this peace?

- **Make the conscious choice not to worry and to replace your thoughts of worry with God's truth.**
- **Take your circumstances to God in prayer.**
- **Trust that God will not only help you, but that He will sustain you.**

The art of positive thinking doesn't come automatically when you surrender your life to Christ. In fact, the enemy may try even harder to influence your thought life once you belong to Jesus. But God's peace will guard your mind, and you can rely on His strength to help you.

In the end, it is up to you to change your thinking. Paul never told the Philippians that God would automatically put positive thoughts in their minds. They had to make the choice to think godly thoughts, and we must make that same choice every day.

OUR MINDS AND THE LAW: UNDERSTANDING YOUR CONSCIENCE

My young daughters are constantly bombarded with messages telling them to do the right thing. Even secular books and television teach them to live by an "inner moral code." The world calls this your conscience. But as believers, are we supposed to listen to our conscience? Is this biblical?

The Ten Commandments were written on stone tablets. The Jewish people had a written Law, a written visual reminder to obey God. Unfortunately, it wasn't enough. The people lived in rebellion towards God for much of the Old Testament (with a few exceptions of course). By the time Jesus came in the first century, the religious teachers of the Law had been corrupted by their own pride. They followed the Law to the letter, but they did so with selfish motives and a heart that longed to show the world (rather than God) how well they could obey.

They not only had pride issues, but many of the Jewish people hid behind the Law. In other words, they felt that God would always be on their side because of their covenant – that their Law would bring them salvation. But Paul made it clear in Romans 2, being a Jew by birth wouldn't save them.

> *For he is not a Jew who is one outwardly, nor is circumcision that which is outward in the flesh. But he is a Jew who is one inwardly; and circumcision is that which is of the heart, by the Spirit, not by the letter; and his praise is not from men, but from God. – Romans 2:28-29*

So why bring up the Law and the old covenant? Aren't we supposed to be discussing how to renew your mind?

Truth: When you are in Christ, you are part of the new covenant. And when you're a part of the new covenant, the Law is no longer written on stone, but in our hearts and minds. (Hebrews 8:7-10)

With the Law written on our hearts by the power of the Holy Spirit, we are equipped with everything we need to be made righteous and to obey God. Those under the old covenant (the Law that was written on stone) did not have the power of the Holy Spirit living within them.

As partakers of the new covenant, we can rely on the Holy Spirit to guide our choices. We can know right from wrong, not because of a written law but because the Holy Spirit is revealing God's truth to us on a daily basis.

The world refers to this "inner moral code" as your conscience. The problem with the world's version of a conscience is that it is relative, which essentially makes it unreliable. It's based on human feelings, and what feels right for one person will feel wrong to another.

But when we rely on the law that God has written in our hearts and minds, we can rest assured that it can be trusted.

So while the world listens to a conscience that is based on feelings, we too listen to our "conscience" – also known as the Holy Spirit.

THE ART OF BIBLICAL MEDITATION

Meditation is nothing new. It's a part of many traditions and religions, and studies have shown it to have great benefits in terms of health and stress levels. Setting aside the fact that it may actually be good for us, many Christians consider it to be sinful. Have you ever wondered why that is?

The answer lies in the simple fact that it is practiced heavily by other religions. Many of these religions use meditation to focus on the mind. They train themselves to control their thoughts, which in turn changes their perception of the world. They are better able to cope with stress, become more compassionate and peaceful people, manage their emotions, and become diligent in their thought life. Sounds all good right?

Now before you write me off, let me explain what's wrong with worldly meditation. Something is missing - and that something is actually a Someone. You see, worldly meditation is all about you. It takes everything that's right with meditating (and there is a right way to meditate, but more on that later), and it removes God from the picture entirely. Worldly meditation places the power, the control, the ability to transform, and the ability to experience peace in the hands of the one who is meditating.

So is there such a thing as biblical meditation? If so, what does it look like in practice?

We first see meditation in the book of Genesis. Isaac was in his field meditating when he first laid eyes on Rebekah. (Genesis 24:62-67) It comes up again in the book of Joshua when God tells the people to "meditate on the Book of the Law day and night."

The principle is simple: your thoughts control your actions. If your mind focused on His Law and His goodness, there will be no room for sin. It will be much easier to say 'no' to temptation.

Meditation is also discussed frequently throughout the Psalms:

Let the words of my mouth and the meditation of my heart be acceptable in Your sight, O Lord, my rock and my Redeemer. - Psalm 19:14

My eyes anticipate the night watches, that I may meditate on Your word. - Psalm 119:148

We aren't just called to meditate on God's Word; we are to also meditate on His love and His promises. In this way, biblical meditation is entirely different from worldly meditation.

The method: Worldly meditation tells you to "empty your mind" or to "let your mind guide your meditation experience." Biblical meditation tells us to focus on God, His Word, and His promises. Instead of emptying our minds we are actually filling our minds continually with Him.

The results: While both promise peace, character transformation, and genuine happiness (or joy), it's a promise that worldly meditation simply cannot keep... at least not fully. And if you do experience some of these things, it's for all the wrong reasons. The only way to experience true peace in EVERY circumstance is to have God's peace which transcends all understanding. And He alone is the true source of joy. And what about character transformation? I'm not going to lie... reading the list of benefits on a meditation website sounds a lot like reading the list of the fruits of the Spirit. Can you genuinely become more patient, kind, and more self-controlled apart from the Holy Spirit? Maybe on the surface... but only the Holy Spirit can offer the real deal.

At first, I found it interesting that the world's version tried to offer things that only God can provide, but then something clicked. Worldly meditation is the enemy's counterfeit of biblical meditation. He took a biblical concept, removed God from the equation, and tried to offer it with the same potential "benefits."

As Christians, we often throw things out that seem "worldly." When meditation became popular, many Christians threw it out in fear that they would somehow be doing something not of God.

But the truth is that meditation belonged to God first. The enemy simply distorted it.

How blessed is the man who does not walk in the counsel of the wicked, nor stand in the path of sinners, nor sit in the seat of scoffers! But his delight is in the law of the Lord, and in His law he meditates day and night. He will be like a tree firmly planted by streams of water, which yields its fruit in its season and its leaf does not wither; and in whatever he does, he prospers. - Psalm 1:1-3

Week 3 Study Guide:

- Read Acts 17:10-11. What made the Berean's "open-minded"? How did they respond to new biblical teaching that was new and unfamiliar?

- Read 2 Corinthians 3:14-16. How does Paul describe the Old Covenant in contrast to our New Covenant in Jesus?

- Read Philippians 4:4-8. In what ways are we called to be positive in our thinking?

- Can you think of a time in your life when you had to *choose* to think differently about your circumstance? What happened as a result of changing your thinking? In what ways can you be proactive in choosing to be positive in your thought life?

- Read Ezekiel 36:26-27. What is the purpose behind putting His law in our hearts rather than on stone?

- Read John 10:3-5. How does this truth reassure you as you strive to be led by the Holy Spirit?

- Read Joshua 1:8. Why is it important to meditate on God's Word, and what are some of the benefits?

- What are some practical ways we can start incorporating biblical meditation into our everyday lives?

Week 4: Guarding Your Mind in Christ

WHAT IT MEANS TO BE DOUBLE-MINDED

What does it mean to be double-minded? As we've discussed throughout this study, your mind and your thought life are crucial. We are called to have the mind of Christ, to meditate on Him and His promises, and to allow the Holy Spirit to transform us from the inside out by the renewing of our minds.

Certainly, there's no room for double-mindedness.

> *But if any of you lacks wisdom, let him ask of God, who gives to all generously and without reproach, and it will be given to him. But he must ask in faith without any doubting, for the one who doubts is like the surf of the sea, driven and tossed by the wind. For that man ought not to expect that he will receive anything from the Lord, being a double-minded man, unstable in all his ways. - James 1:5-8*

In this passage from the book of James, we see a double-minded man. Part of his mind believes that God will give him what he asks for (wisdom), and the other part of his mind doubts that God will keep His promise. In this case, his "double mind" consists of both faith and doubt.

I don't know about you, but I found this passage to be quite convicting. I think we've all experienced our fair share of doubt over the years, and having absolute faith and zero doubt 100% of the time seems next to impossible. But this verse is pretty clear: one who doubts God's faithfulness is "unstable in all they do."

There is one other place in the book of James where we are warned of double-mindedness:

> *Submit therefore to God. Resist the devil and he will flee from you. Draw near to God and He will draw near to you. Cleanse your hands, you sinners; and purify your hearts, you double-minded. - James 4:7-8*

In this instance, being double-minded has to do with worldly thinking and sin. We can't serve two masters.

We can't be double-minded - thinking like the world and striving to have the mind of Christ simultaneously. It simply doesn't work.

In all honesty, both passages define the "double-minded man" as someone who tries to serve God yet still thinks like the world. In one instance, he doubts God and His promises. He lives by sight rather than by faith. And in the other instance, he allows the enemy to guide his thinking. He lives like the world while trying to serve God.

By biblical standards, a double-minded man is one who has been given the mind of Christ, but he isn't operating in it. He's constantly going back and forth. This is why the Bible calls him unstable.

So don't be double-minded. Choose instead to be single-minded, throwing away worldly thinking. *Never forget that you have been given the mind of Christ, so use it.*

GUARD YOUR MIND: HOW TO BE PROACTIVE IN YOUR THOUGHT LIFE

For most of my life, I just let my mind do its thing. Thoughts were thoughts. I couldn't control them - right? Wrong. Not only is it possible to change your thinking, we are commanded to do so as believers. But it doesn't happen overnight. Renewing your mind towards Christ is a daily (sometimes minute to minute) process. And it starts by learning how to guard your mind.

Let me ask you a question: Is it easier to break a long-term habit or to prevent that habit from taking root in the first place? You see, your mind often operates out of habit or routine, and dwelling on negative thoughts becomes a habit rather quickly. Wouldn't it be easier to guard your mind and prevent the pattern of negative thinking in the first place?

So I must ask — what are you doing to be proactive? How are you guarding your mind?

Here are a few practical ways to guard your mind against unwanted thinking:

- **Pay attention to what you watch and what you listen to.**

Remember the song "Oh Be Careful Little Eyes What You See?" One of the best ways to guard your mind is to not fill it with junk. Philippians 4:8 tells us to think about what is true, noble, right, pure, lovely, admirable, excellent, and praiseworthy. Are you watching things that cause you to think this way? What about music? Is what you're listening to "excellent and praiseworthy"?

The best way to think godly thoughts is to protect your mind from things that aren't godly.

- **Guard your mind against the spirit of fear.**

I had a friend who struggled with nightmares - so much so that she was afraid to go to sleep at night. As a married woman, when her husband was out of town, she would stay at her parents' house because she was afraid to be alone in her own house. But this young woman was also a major fan of horror films - the scarier the better. She watched them regularly believing that they had no effect on her thinking.

Truth: Everything you subject your mind to will ultimately affect your thought life.

There's one more aspect of fear I'd like to mention - one that is rather subtle. When you're watching the news or reading the newspaper, do you ever feel afraid? Our world likes to spread shocking news, and nothing sells a news story better than fear. If you're constantly filling your mind with bad news and all of the reasons why you should be afraid, are you really guarding your mind?

Aren't we supposed to focus on the truth of the unseen rather than the seen? It's certainly not a bad thing to read the news, but do so with a guarded mind and the right perspective.

- **Guard your mind against sinful thoughts.**

Yes, it is true that the enemy will plant seeds of doubt, fear, and sin into our minds. We can't prevent every negative thought. Even Jesus experienced temptation while fasting in the desert. But we can certainly be

25

proactive in coming against the enemy's lies. We do this by arming ourselves with the truth. A seed can only grow if it's watered and fed. So don't water and feed the enemy's lies. And when you recognize a seed planted by the enemy, know that you have the authority to uproot it with the truth.

Not every seed planted by the enemy is an obvious sin. More often than not, they are subtle. We are tempted to be afraid, to worry, to doubt, or to think we're unworthy. These are the most dangerous schemes of all because they affect our thought life the most.

SOBER-MINDED: KEEPING YOUR MIND ALERT

Obviously the first thought to come to mind in terms of the word "sober" is abstaining from alcohol. But is that what the Bible is telling us? Is it telling us not to drink? I personally believe that the biblical definition of being sober-minded goes beyond abstaining from drunkenness. We are called to keep our minds alert and prepared for action. In fact, the Bible speaks of our "sober" mind most often in the case of warfare.

Be of sober spirit, be on the alert. Your adversary, the devil, prowls around like a roaring lion, seeking someone to devour. - 1 Peter 5:8

We're called to be alert because we have a very real enemy. And even though Jesus already defeated him on the cross, he is constantly trying to sabotage God's plans and our call to advance the Kingdom. Keep in mind, the enemy cannot hurt you. He cannot steal your salvation or "pluck you out of the Father's hand." But he can try to inhibit your growth. He can try to deceive you and render you useless in the Kingdom. And he can certainly try to keep you from spreading the Good News to the world.

We are told to be sober-minded and alert because when we are constantly on guard, the enemy doesn't stand a chance.

All actions originate in the mind. I've heard it said that when you commit a sin, you actually commit the sin twice - once in your thought life and then again when you act on those thoughts. Remember it was Jesus who said that even looking at another person (who is not your spouse) with lust in your heart is adultery. When it comes to righteous living, your thoughts matter!

What if we seriously took control of our thought life? What if we took every negative thought captive and made them obey Christ? (2 Corinthians 10:5) Our lives would never be the same.

When it comes to battle, we have to be alert. If you were a soldier on the front lines in the middle of intense warfare, would you for one second take your mind off of what you were doing? Of course not! (And if you did, you'd probably be a dead man.)

Be alert. Don't let anything influence your thinking or distract you from your mission.

This is what it means to be sober-minded.

BE PREPARED: WHY YOU SHOULD KNOW GOD'S WORD WELL

What would you do if you were wrongly accused of a crime? You're on trial and about to appear before a judge and jury with your testimony of events. How would you respond? What steps would you take to be prepared to testify?

I'm an organized, to-do-list kind of girl. So I would probably have a binder full of documents, pieces of evidence, and whatever else I needed to present my case fully to the jury. I would be as prepared as a person possibly could be.

To say that the early church was greatly persecuted is a vast understatement. Paul was put on trial, persecuted, and imprisoned throughout his ministry. He was even stoned at one point and dragged outside the city assumed to be dead. (Acts 14:19-20) The church was "eager to do good" but often suffered for their choice to follow Christ and spread His message. In the midst of being threatened, they were told to be prepared to share their reason for hope – and not with anger or force, but with gentleness and respect.

I'm not sure what I would need to be prepared for most - having an answer to give or speaking that answer in truth and love.

In order to be prepared to share the truth, we must be willing to study the truth as well as apply the truth to our own lives. In this way, we are able to share the truth in love.

We share the truth the same way Jesus did - love first and teach second. The two cannot be separated.

It's not enough to know the Bible well. In order to teach others, we have to be living examples of what the Bible teaches. That's why it's so important to not only be in the Word, but to also be spending time with God in prayer.

As followers of Jesus, we must be prepared. Our words alone won't suffice as evidence for Christ; rather the best evidence involves our actions and unconditional love for others. The world can argue our words, but there's no arguing a life filled with good deeds and love for the world.

It's not enough to know the Word; we have to live the Word. And the best way to live the Word is to know it well.

Week 4 Study Guide:

- Read Luke 17:5-6. How did Jesus respond when the disciples asked Him to increase their faith? How does this give you hope in your own faith?

- Read 1 Corinthians 2:12-16. What does it mean to have "the mind of Christ"?

- According to Proverbs 4:23 and Luke 6:45, why is it important to guard your heart and mind?

- How does focusing on the unseen rather than the seen help us to guard our minds?

- Read 1 Peter 1:13-16. What does this passage tell us to do in addition to being sober-minded?

- According to Ephesians 6:18, what is the best way to remain sober-minded?

- Read 1 Peter 3:13-16. Why is it important to be prepared with answers as to why we believe what we believe?

- According to 2 Timothy 4:2-5, why was Timothy urged to be prepared? What are some practical ways we can be prepared in the same way?

Week 5: Truth vs Reality

FOCUSING ON THE UNSEEN TRUTH

It's all about perspective.

I've heard this phrase countless times, and yet I often need to be reminded of its truth. When we encounter a difficult situation, we can choose to see things differently – through new eyes. If we would simply change our perspective, we can change how we feel about any given situation.

I've heard it said that we as Christians should see things through an eternal perspective. But what does that mean exactly? How do we go about seeing the world through "eternal" eyes?

First, I'd like to point out what it doesn't mean. In an effort to escape the pain and struggle of this life, it's easy to focus on heaven and our eternity with Jesus. And we should look forward to the glorious hope we have of spending eternity with our heavenly Father! **But it is possible to become so eternity-minded that you become no earthly good.**

We were meant to be present in this life. God has amazing plans for us and divine encounters that He's called us to fulfill. We all have people we were destined to reach, and conversations that were meant to be had. We don't want to become so anxious to leave this life, that we don't live it to the fullest.

Life on this planet is a gift. I'm not saying that it isn't hard. And sometimes it can be downright painful. But through the pain and struggle, we get to experience God's provision. We learn to trust Him, our faith grows, and we become more mature as children of God. Am I excited for heaven? You bet! (And that's definitely an understatement!!) But I also know I have a purpose here in this life. And I want to be able to say that I fought the good fight and did all that God called me to do while I was here.

So now that we know what having an eternal perspective isn't, let's talk about what it is – seeing life through the eyes of our Father.

As Christians, we have been given the mind of Christ. And for this reason, we strive to see His plan for our lives rather than the struggles we are currently facing. When we look at others, we make an effort to see them the way God sees them, with unconditional love. We see things from His perspective rather than our own.

Our lives are so busy and noisy that we often struggle to slow down and pay attention to what is really going on. We become so completely engrossed with our earthly tasks, that we fail to see what God is doing behind the scenes. We need to look up and be alert. **God is always working, always moving.**

Focus on the unseen rather than the seen – see the world and our circumstances the way God sees them.

So as we strive to renew our minds, one of the best ways to do so is to make a conscious effort to slow down and change our perspective. Maybe then we can experience the peace that comes along with knowing how much God cares for us and that He is always working things together for the good of those who love Him.

...While we look not at the things which are seen, but at the things which are not seen; for the things which are seen are temporal, but the things which are not seen are eternal. – 2 Corinthians 4:18

---

6 THINGS TO SPEND YOUR TIME THINKING ABOUT

If someone were to ask you to describe your thought life, what would you say? Is it deliberate and intentional? Do you entertain thoughts and ideas you shouldn't? How much time do you spend each day worrying about your to-do list or day-to-day activities? Or maybe your thoughts are consumed with your job, your kids, or your hobby.

The truth is that everyone has a thought life; and according to the Bible, it's important. Your thoughts matter. They have the power to inspire action and change in your life. But they can also cripple you and keep you from your calling.

Your mind is a powerful thing indeed. It was created by God for many purposes. We meditate, make decisions, imagine, create, organize, worship, pray... and the list goes on. So yes, your thought life matters. And it is up to us to be deliberate about how we choose to think.

Finally, brethren, whatever is true, whatever is honorable, whatever is right, whatever is pure, whatever is lovely, whatever is of good repute, if there is any excellence and if anything worthy of praise, dwell on these things. – Philippians 4:8

Whatever is true… Do we fill our mind with true statements? Are we truth-seekers? It's so important to fill our minds with the truth when we have a very real enemy who is literally described as the father of lies. Spiritually speaking, Jesus identified Himself as the truth, and we certainly need to be filling our minds with Him. But we also need to make sure we are truth-seekers in other areas of our life. Are we believing the world's lies about who we are and what we need to be? Are we buying in to the lies of the enemy that our prayers don't matter?

Whatever is honorable… An honorable person is one who is honest, both in public and in private. How would you feel if your thought life were on public display? Would you be proud of your thoughts? Would they be worthy of honor?

Whatever is right… To have "right" thoughts simply means to think righteously. Is your thought life in line with God's Word? Would they be acceptable by God's standards? We can't allow sin to creep its way into our thoughts.

Whatever is pure… In the same way that we are called to have "just" thoughts, they should be pure, clean and innocent as well.

Whatever is lovely… It's amazing how God calls us to think lovely thoughts. It's so easy to be consumed by our to-do lists that we fail to take time to think about all things beautiful.

Whatever is of good repute… How do we think of others? Do we point out their flaws and weaknesses? We are called to think kindly towards each other, to see their potential in Christ, and to love unconditionally.

The Bible is clear on one major point concerning our thought life: We decide how to think.

God wouldn't have commanded us to replace our worldly thoughts with godly thoughts if it was an impossible task. He also wouldn't have commanded it if we didn't play an active role in making it happen.

God won't change our minds for us, but He will be faithful to reveal to us the areas that need to change. It is up to us to make the necessary changes (with the Holy Spirit's help of course.)

So start being intentional about your thoughts. Think about what you're thinking about. If your thoughts were on display for the world to see, would the world describe them the way Philippians 4:8 describes the mind of a believer? Or would changes be in order?

I speak from experience when I say that changing your thought life is hard. It's a life-long process to say the least. But I do know that it is worth it because everything we do for God is worth it.

UNDERSTANDING YOUR PLACE IN CHRIST

The Bible has a lot to say about us as children of God. We are new creations, royal priests, set free from sin, partakers of Christ's divine nature, and co-heirs with Christ. It even tells us that we are currently seated with Christ in heavenly places! But when we look around at this world, it can be difficult to claim this truth. We see ourselves still struggling with sin, we face tragedies and hardships. We don't feel like new creations. Many things still feel old.

So what's the truth?

As a child of God, you have been given the Holy Spirit. You were reborn on the day of your salvation. The old life is gone, and the new life has begun. On the outside, however, you look exactly the same. Walking down the street, no one would know that you are now an adopted son or daughter of the Creator. They can't visibly see the Holy Spirit living inside of you.

But I'd like to pose an important question:

Which is more true – who you are in the physical realm or who you are in Christ?

He is the image of the invisible God, the firstborn of all creation. For by Him all things we[re] created, both in the heavens and on earth, visible and invisible, whether thrones or dominio[ns] rulers or authorities—all things have been created through Him and for Him. He is before all [things] and in Him all things hold together. – Colossians 1:15-17

It's hard to imagine the unseen world. But the Bible describes it as a created place with "thrones, kingdoms, rulers, and authorities." Honestly, my first thought while reading this passage was that this realm must be pretty massive if it contains entire kingdoms!

Jesus was God in the flesh. We could see Him in our physical realm. But to the world, He was simply a man. He looked just like everyone else. The Bible says there was nothing attractive about Him, nothing that screamed, "It's me! I'm the Messiah!" But that wasn't the truth. He wasn't just an ordinary man. He was the Son of God. His reality, His truth, was unseen.

When we are born of the Spirit, our truth, our reality in Christ, is also unseen.

We may look the same as everyone else in this physical world, but we are not the same. We are alive! And not only are we alive, but we are living out our God-given purpose through the power of the Holy Spirit. Our Father is using us to display His wisdom and grace to the unseen world. (That's quite a calling!)

Your reality is not bound by this physical world. You were born of the Spirit.

And what is true in the Spirit is far more real than what is true in the natural.

Therefore we do not lose heart, but though our outer man is decaying, yet our inner man is being renewed day by day. For momentary, light affliction is producing for us an eternal weight of glory far beyond all comparison. – 2 Corinthians 4:16-17

---

4 PRACTICAL WAYS TO RID YOURSELF OF WORRY

Why do we worry so much? Honestly, I worry about the craziest things sometimes. I worry about my relationships, my safety, my finances, what to make for dinner… I seriously don't know why I devote so much of my time and attention to worry. Well… maybe I do know. Worry is simply a lack of trust.

There are certain things my children never worry about. They never worry if they'll have food to eat for breakfast or if they will have clothes to wear tomorrow. They never worry about finances or getting good grades in school. At 3 and 5 years old, they have no idea what it's like to worry about these things. Why? Because they trust. They trust that mommy and daddy will take care of them. And if they experience sadness or they fall and hurt themselves? We are there to pick them up and nurture them back to health, both physically and emotionally.

As adults, we worry much more than our children. We suddenly have responsibilities. We have bills to pay and mouths to feed. After experiencing heartache and brokenness of our own, we learn that sometimes people can't be trusted. We've been let down, and we ourselves have let others down as well. So needless to say, there's much more to worry about.

What if we really had the faith of a child? What if we trusted God with everything in our lives the way our children trust us? He is our heavenly Father after all. And unlike human beings, He is incapable of failing us. He will never ever let us down. Our Father can be trusted in a way that no human being can be trusted.

So what does this all have to do with renewing your mind? If you're anything like me, worry has a way of consuming your thought life. And when your thoughts are consumed with worry, they can't be consumed with anything else. Jesus told us in Matthew 6 to "seek first His kingdom and His righteousness." And it's impossible for His Kingdom to consume your thoughts when you're worried!

The solution to worry is simple: learn to trust.

- **Say it out loud.** "God, I trust You. I trust you with my life, my career, my family, my finances… everything. God, I trust You with everything."

- **Dive into the Scriptures.** Remind yourselves of God's faithfulness throughout time – the times He took care of His children even when things looked grim.

- **Keep a prayer journal.** Writing down your prayers gives you a reference point. As you look back at your prayers, you'll be able to see God at work. You'll be reminded that He always has your best interest at heart.

- **Declare His promises.** God is faithful. He is the same yesterday, today, and forever. Remind yourselves of this truth each and every day. God can indeed be trusted – with the big stuff and the small stuff. He cares about it all.

hen I am afraid, I will put my trust in You. In God, whose word I praise, in God I have put my trust; I shall not be afraid. What can mere man do to me? – Psalm 56:3-4

Week 5 Study Guide:

- Read Colossians 3:1-2. What are we called to seek and set our minds on? What are some examples of things we should and should not focus on?

- What do you suppose 2 Corinthians 4:18 means when it tells us to fix our eyes on the "unseen"?

- Read Philippians 3:13-15. What are we called to focus on and what hope do we find in verse 15 if we are struggling in our thought life?

- Read Romans 8:5-6. What choice do we have to make concerning our thought life, and what are the results of that choice?

- Read Colossians 3:1-4. In verses 1-2 we are told to set our minds on "things above" rather than on earthly things. In your own words, describe the reason why we are called to do this based on verses 3-4.

- Read Ephesians 2:6-7 and 3:10-11. What is our role as believers in the unseen heavenly realms?

- Read Matthew 6:28-34. What reasons did Jesus give for why we shouldn't worry about our basic needs?

- Why do you suppose Jesus told us to seek His Kingdom first while speaking of practical worries? In other words, how does seeking His Kingdom prevent us from worrying in this life?

Week 6: When Your Identity Changes the Way You Think

WHAT IT MEANS TO BE THE CHILD OF A GOOD FATHER

What is your perception of God? If you had to describe your Creator, what would you say? For many who don't know Him, God seems distant. They will say things like, "God, if you're out there..." But we know that He isn't far away. He hears our prayers, knows our thoughts, and cares about the smallest details of our lives. He's a good, good Father, and we are His beloved children.

I often wonder if we struggle to get past the God of the Old Testament. He seems to be quite angry... a lot. We read about judgment and wrath. We see His people suffering the consequences of their choices by being exiled, losing battles, and wandering in the desert for 40 years. This is a picture that many non-believers have of God. You have to love Him and obediently serve Him, or He will send you straight to hell.

Growing up, I had a similar image: To the Father, I was awful, unworthy of salvation, and destined to receive His wrath. I pictured the God of the Old Testament unleashing His anger. Then Jesus came and made things right between me and God, taking God's wrath for me on the cross.

I subconsciously envisioned the Father and the Son with two different personalities. I knew deep down that I was wrong to think this way, but for some reason, I couldn't shake the image of an angry Old Testament Father and a loving New Testament Son. But the truth is that if we have seen the Son, we've seen the Father. The love and compassion Jesus showed is an *exact representation* of our loving and compassionate Father.

For God so loved the world...

The Father loves us deeply and unconditionally. If His love were conditional, the Bible would say "For God so loved the ones that accepted Jesus." No. It says that He loves the world... the whole world... all mankind.

That's why He wants to adopt all of us. Think about that for a minute. His desire is to adopt every single one of us as His own.

Blessed be the God and Father of our Lord Jesus Christ, who has blessed us with every spiritual blessing in the heavenly places in Christ, just as He chose us in Him before the foundation of the world, that we would be holy and blameless before Him. In love He predestined us to adoption as sons through Jesus Christ to Himself, according to the kind intention of His will, to the praise of the glory of His grace, which He freely bestowed on us in the Beloved. - Ephesians 1:3-6

The Greek word used in this passage for "adoption as sons" was a legal term. In Roman culture, it referred to the full legal standing of an adopted male heir. The same Greek term is used in Romans 8.

God's purpose in saving us through the cross goes far beyond the forgiveness of sins. He wants to adopt us. And not just adopt us but make us legal heirs.

In Christ, we inherit the earth, the kingdom, *and* eternal life. (Matthew 5:2-11)

As our good, good Father, God desires the very best for our lives.

He longs to have a deep and meaningful relationship with us. He doesn't want to be distant, He desires to be close - the way the best of fathers would be with their children.

DETERMINING YOUR WORTH: IS SELF-ESTEEM BIBLICAL?

How do you see yourself? Are you worth it? These are questions our culture asks on a regular basis. My preschool daughters are constantly receiving messages through media about the importance of a strong self-esteem and how we should believe in ourselves. But is it scriptural to "believe in yourself?"

Let me pose a question: When it comes to retail, how is price determined? If I were to drive to the mall right now and purchase a shirt, how much would I pay? Well, it would depend on a lot of factors. Am I purchasing this shirt from a high-end store or a store known for its "good deals?" Is the shirt on sale or on clearance maybe? How well-made is it? Is it casual or dressy?

Here's the bottom line: The shirt would cost whatever someone was willing to pay for it.

When clothes move to the clearance rack, it's because they need to lower the price so that someone will actually buy it. Maybe the shirt isn't in style anymore or maybe it's out of season. Or perhaps it just didn't sell for one reason or another.

Now let me ask you another question: How much are you worth?

But God demonstrates His own love toward us, in that while we were yet sinners, Christ died for us.
- Romans 5:8

Jesus paid everything for you with no guarantee that you would accept His gift of salvation - that's how much you are worth.

Have you ever paid more for something because it was a name-brand? Maybe you paid twice as much for a designer purse simply because it had the name of a famous designer on it. This may seem like a silly analogy, but it couldn't be truer.

You were designed by God and created in His image. You are adorned with the logo of your Creator. *Do you understand how valuable that makes you?*

In the church, we are often taught that good self-esteem equals pride and that low self-esteem equals humility, but this couldn't be further from the truth. Jesus didn't die for your sins and bless you with every spiritual blessing so that you could wallow in how sinful you used to be. We see ourselves as so unworthy, but the truth is that God doesn't see you that way. We are His beloved children, and He longs to see us reach our potential. He wants to see us thrive and be the people He created us to be.

If God sees us as valuable, loved, and cherished sons and daughters, why do we choose to see ourselves as anything less?

I think in our attempt to be humble, we've made ourselves worthless. But that's not humility. Yes, we recognize our need for a Savior, but that doesn't mean we beat ourselves up and put ourselves down.

It's all about putting things in perspective. You are valuable because you were designed in His image. God made you worthy of salvation through His Son Jesus Christ, and He did this <u>before</u> you cleaned up your act. You have been declared righteous and washed clean by the blood of the Lamb.

So let's stop seeing ourselves as we used to be, and start seeing ourselves the way Jesus did when He looked at us and said, "You're worth it."

HUMILITY VS SELF-DEFEAT: LESSONS FROM OUR SAVIOR

Let me ask you a question: Was Jesus humble? Did He exhibit pride in any of His behavior? I think we can all agree that Jesus is our perfect example of true humility. Paul certainly agreed in his letter to the Philippians:

Have this attitude in yourselves which was also in Christ Jesus, who, although He existed in the form of God, did not regard equality with God a thing to be grasped, but emptied Himself, taking the form of a bond-servant, and being made in the likeness of men. Being found in appearance as a man, He humbled Himself by becoming obedient to the point of death, even death on a cross. For this reason also, God highly exalted Him, and bestowed on Him the name which is above every name, so that at the name of Jesus every knee will bow, of those who are in heaven and on earth and under the earth, and that every tongue will confess that Jesus Christ is Lord, to the glory of God the Father. - Philippians 2:5-11

Three truths about humility that were exhibited by Jesus:

- **True humility involves becoming a servant.**

This is what Jesus did when He came to die for our sins. He even demonstrated his humble character when He washed the feet of the disciples. When we consider the needs of others above our own (Philippians 2:3-4), we are demonstrating a true servant's heart. And while this may seem counter-cultural in a world that teaches us to take care of our own needs first, this servant-like attitude is what Jesus conveyed to the world when He left His riches in heaven to be born in a manger and serve us willingly with His life.

- **True humility means having an obedient heart.**

In Philippians, Paul tells us that Jesus "humbled himself by becoming obedient to the point of death." Do we have an obedient heart? Or does my heart long to rebel? When my daughters choose to obey me it's because they are choosing to be humble, but when they disobey it's as if they are saying, "No. I want to do it MY way." In essence, this is the very definition of pride. My way is better. But humility says, "Your way is better." And we all know deep down that God's way is ALWAYS better.

- **True humility means knowing where your gifts and talents come from and understanding your place in the body of believers.**

In Romans 12:3-8, Paul reminds us not to think of ourselves more highly than we are and to use "sober judgment" when we take a look at our lives. In context, he's talking about our place in the body of Christ.

He was addressing believers who were saying that certain gifts of the Spirit were superior to others - that in the body, some parts were simply more important. To be humble, however, means recognizing that God values every one of His children the same. It doesn't matter how you serve Him, you are crucial to the body of Christ.

My daughter has a favorite blanket - her "Pooh blankie." This thing is carried around the house day and night. She never leaves home without it. To her, this blanket means everything. The other day, she spilled chocolate milk all over it. It was dirty and needed to be washed. (And if you're a mom, you know the battle I faced trying to convince her to give up her blanket for an hour or two so it could be washed! Tears. Lots and lots of tears.) Dirty or not, that blanket still held its value to my little girl. She loved it no less even though it was dirty.

Even when you were dirty with sin, God LOVED you. In His eyes, you still held your value. You were dirty and in need of a Savior, but He still beheld you as His beloved creation.

Humility is never self-loathing. It never says, "I'm worth nothing." You were dirty, and your attempts to be righteous on your own couldn't make you clean. But you were still loved by God, so much so that He sent His Son to die so that you could be washed by the blood of the Lamb.

In our attempt to be humble as Christians, it's easy to put ourselves down. We say things like, "God you are everything, and I am nothing." And while it's true that God is everything; it's not true that you are nothing. If you were nothing, why did Jesus die for you? If you were worthless, why go through all that pain and suffering?

You bear the image of God. He saw you as a person of value even *before* you turned to Him as your Savior. Perhaps a better thing to say would be, "God, you are everything, and I am humbled by Your love for me. Here I am, your servant, ready and willing to be used by You and to be obedient to Your call on my life."

WHAT THE BIBLE SAYS ABOUT YOU (AND WHAT IT DOESN'T)

Our new identity in Christ is something I am very passionate about. In our church today, I hear so many Christians speak poorly about themselves, and it truly saddens me. I must admit that I used to be one of them. I used to believe that I was a lowly, undeserving sinner. How could God possibly want me? How could He use someone like me? Weren't there people out there who were more "qualified" in the eyes of God?

And then I started learning about my identity as God's child. You see, I used to be a sinner, but I'm not a sinner anymore. I'm a child of the living God. And if you're a believer, the same is true of you.

Here's a list of just <u>some</u> of the good things God has to say about you in His Word:

- You have been adopted into God's family – you are His child and He is your good, good Father. (John 1:12)

- Jesus considers you a friend, not a servant or slave. (John 15:15)

- You have been justified and redeemed by Christ (Romans 3:24)

- Your old nature was crucified with Christ, and you are no longer a slave to sin. (Romans 6:6)

- As a child of God, you are a co-heir with Christ. (Romans 8:17)

- The Holy Spirit lives within you, making you God's temple. (1 Corinthians 6:19)

- You are united with Christ. (1 Corinthians 6:17)

- You are a new creation in Christ. (2 Corinthians 5:17)

- You have become the righteousness of God. (2 Corinthians 5:21)

- You are no longer a slave, but God's child and His heir. (Galatians 4:7)

- You have been set free in Christ. (Galatians 5:1)

- You have been blessed with every spiritual blessing in the heavenly places. (Ephesians 1:3)

- You are chosen, holy, and blameless before God. (Ephesians 1:4)

- You have been sealed with the Holy Spirit. (Ephesians 1:13)

- You are alive with Christ. (Ephesians 2:4-5)

- You are seated with Christ in the heavenly places. (Ephesians 2:6)

- You are God's masterpiece created to accomplish good works. (Ephesians 2:10)

- You are a member of God's family and a partaker of His promise. (Ephesians 3:6)

- You were formerly darkness, but now you are children of the light. (Ephesians 5:8)

- You are a citizen of heaven. (Philippians 3:20)

- God's peace guards your heart and mind. (Philippians 4:7)

- God supplies your needs (Philippians 4:19)

- You are complete in Christ Jesus. (Colossians 2:10)

- You are victorious. (1 John 5:4-5)

This list isn't even complete and already I'm overwhelmed at how much God has given us. What a transformation! I once was a sinner, but now I am everything on that list and more. *This realization changed my life.*

I needed to stop calling myself by my old identity and start claiming my new identity in Christ!

I've searched the New Testament high and low. I could not find one verse that claimed we were still sinners *after* our adoption into the family of God. In fact, I found many verses that tell us how sin no longer has any power in our lives, that all we have to do is resist the devil and he runs away, and that our sin nature was actually crucified with Christ... meaning it's dead.

To claim that I'm still a sinner is to claim that my sin nature isn't dead, that it still has power, and that I will always "struggle" with sin. *How can we "struggle" against a dead man?*

I truly believe that the reason we still struggle with sin is because we believe the lie of the enemy that says we still have to struggle. He's an identity thief - remember? He wants you to believe that the chains of sin are still there and that you are still addicted to your past life.

Why would God tell us there is ALWAYS a way out of temptation if there wasn't ALWAYS a way out for us? Greater is He that is in me than He that is in the world - right?

The New Testament writers were constantly reminding the new believers of their identity in Christ. They needed to remember that they now had the resurrection power of the Holy Spirit living inside of them. I truly believe it was because they struggled with many of the same lies we still deal with today.

Are you really who God says you are?

It's time we started saying, "Yes. I am exactly who God says I am." Because when we start to believe this truth, the enemy runs in fear of what we can and will do in the name of Jesus.

Week 6 Study Guide:

- What do we learn about the nature of Christ in Hebrews 1:3?

- Read Romans 8:15-17. How do we know that we are truly children of God? What are we promised to receive as His children?

- Read Matthew 5:2-11. What did Jesus say we would inherit as children of God?

- Read Psalm 139:13-15. What comfort do you find in knowing that you were so intricately made by your Creator?

- According to Philippians 2:3-4, what does it mean to be humble? What do you suppose keeps us from being humble in this way?

- Read Romans 12:3-21. What does Paul urge us to do as believers with the gifts God has given us? According to verses 9-21, how do we put these gifts to use while remaining humble?

- What happens when we start to question our identity in Christ? Why do you suppose we question it and what can we do to stand firm in who we are?

- What lie do you personally struggle with most when it comes to your identity? Identity and share a Scripture that you can cling to when you feel this way about yourself.

Week 7: War of the Mind

THE REAL BATTLEFIELD

The New Testament reminds us quite often that we are in a battle. The enemy is a liar, and his goal is to take you down. Now he certainly can't steal you away from God, but he can hinder your walk. If you believe his lies, he can keep you from advancing the kingdom, living the call on your life, and from being all that God intended you to be here on earth. I truly believe this is why God calls us to renew our minds daily in Him. Because when all is said and done, the real battlefield - the place where we fight the enemy and his lies - occurs in the mind.

How does the enemy lie to you? In my experience, he plants thoughts. Think of your mind like a garden. In the garden of your mind, the enemy scatters seeds - doubts, insecurities, fear, lies, and temptations. Before we had the truth and the power of the Holy Spirit, there wasn't much we could do about these seeds. We were slaves to sin. And without the Holy Spirit, we undoubtedly didn't even realize these seeds were being planted in the first place.

But now our eyes are open. We can clearly see the enemy's lies, and we can identify the enemy's seeds before they have a chance to take root. We don't have to allow these seeds to stick around and grow into weeds, rather we can choose to fill our garden with truth instead.

So like I said, your mind is a battlefield. But the Bible makes one thing clear: the fight isn't fair. The darkness has no power over the light. Greater is He that is in you than he that is in the world. The battle is already won, and your victory is secure.

So what does a battle look like that has already been won?

Spiritual warfare comes down to a battle between truth and lies.

Did God really say that?

You aren't really set free from that.

You'll always struggle with that sin.

Why would God want you for that task?

Did God really promise you that?

47

Why can't you be more like that person over there? They have it all together.

This trial you're currently enduring is never going to end. You're always going to suffer.

God's Word says that all things are possible, but come on... you have to be realistic.

There's no way God can do that in your life.

Do any of these lies sound familiar?

In the Garden of Eden, Eve believed lies just like these. The enemy caused Eve to question God's Word and that was that. She bought into the lie (as did Adam) and things were changed forever.

This is why renewing your mind is so crucial. Our minds need to be prepared for the battle.

My husband is quite passionate about his yard. He likes a green, weed-feed yard. (Don't we all?) The one thing he has learned, however, is that the best way to keep weeds away is to keep them from growing in the first place. Weed killers work, but if your grass is thick and healthy enough, they'll choke out most of the weeds naturally. And when a weed does sneak in? It's best to pull it right away making sure to pull the root out as well. Otherwise, it will come back year after year and spread its seeds across your yard creating even more weeds.

My point in all this is to say that when the enemy tries to plant weeds, pull them right away! Don't let them grow. And certainly, don't allow them to scatter new seed! Fill your mind with so much truth that lies have no place.

Since your mind is the real battlefield, always be armed and ready.

We uproot the enemies lies with the truth of God's Word, so the more we know it, the better we will be at the battle.

HOW TO MAKE YOUR THOUGHTS OBEY CHRIST
(AND WHY IT'S IMPORTANT)

I've always been a worrier. I'll admit it. My thoughts often get the best of me. Maybe it's the fact that like to have everything planned out. I need to know what's going to happen and when. And even though I say I like surprises, I actually don't handle them well. Why? Because I'm a bit of a control freak. Yes, I said it. I, Alyssa J Howard, like to be in control.

I've always known that I shouldn't worry. After all, the Bible says so - right? But I don't think it really hit me until I saw some of the same "worry" traits in my oldest daughter. She's always been that way for as long as I can remember. As a young toddler she would organize her toys by color and size (which was very cute at the time!) But now that's she's older, her toys *must* be organized and in their place or she can't fall asleep at night. She gets that from me. Watching her worry about such small details made me realize that I needed to change.

It's not enough that I strive to obey Christ in my actions; my thoughts need to obey Him as well.

We are destroying speculations and every lofty thing raised up against the knowledge of God, and we are taking every thought captive to the obedience of Christ. - 2 Corinthians 10:5

Worry is a sin. So is worldly thinking. And I'm guilty of both on a regular basis. And when I say worldly thinking, I'm not talking about obvious sins and temptations. I'm referring to my to-do list. Every day my mind is consumed with everything I have to accomplish - dishes, laundry, food preparations, errands... even my Bible study becomes something to check off on my to-do list. I don't have time to think about the things of God, the unseen and the eternal, because I spend all of my time thinking about my responsibilities.

Now I'm not saying that we should neglect our day-to-day tasks, but what I am saying is that they shouldn't consume our thoughts.

What consumes your thought life? What do you think about most?

Here's the truth: We have the power to make our thoughts obey the Messiah. We don't have to allow our thoughts to take control, rather we can take control of our thoughts.

1. **Learn to recognize the thoughts that are out of line.** Identifying "disobedient" thoughts is that first step to taking them captive. Worry, fear, doubt, temptation - we need to be proactive in recognizing that these types of thoughts are not of God.

2. **Replace disobedient thoughts with obedient ones.** When we take thoughts captive, we are literally capturing them and forcing them to change. As 2 Corinthians 10:5 tells us, we *make them* obey Christ.

Instead of worrying about finances, I change my thinking and remember that Jesus promised to meet my physical needs. If I'm facing an illness, I remind myself that I serve the Healer. Rather than thinking about everything that could go wrong, I speak the truth of God's Word into my situation.

I take every thought prisoner and make them obey my Savior.

UNDERSTANDING THE TRUTH THAT YOU LACK NOTHING IN CHRIST

Temptations. We all face them. Even Jesus faced His share of temptation. Throughout the Bible, we see people give in to temptation and others who remain strong. We see the repercussions of sin as well as the rewards for saying no to it. As Christians, we know and understand fully that sin is never good for us. It's always better to say no to temptation. But unfortunately, the enemy likes to deceive us into thinking otherwise.

The Bible has quite a bit to say about sin and temptation. Here are four biblical truths:

- **If left unchecked, temptation can lead us into a trap which ultimately leads to ruin. (1 Timothy 6:9)**

- **God never tempts His children. (James 1:13-15)**

- **God <u>always</u> provides a way out of temptation. (1 Corinthians 10:13)**

- **Jesus understands temptation and promises to help us endure. (Hebrews 2:17-18)**

When we think of temptation, we often associate it with "big" sins like adultery, cheating, lying, etc. But the enemy is slyer than that. He's not going to tempt you to steal a car if you've never stolen anything in your life. So by its very definition, it wouldn't be a temptation at all. Real temptations are designed to entice you in some way. And the enemy likes to personalize his attacks.

Temptations are enticing because they promise us something we feel we are currently lacking.

I feel hurt and frustrated... so I'm tempted to lash out and hurt others.

I'm feeling insecure about myself... so I am tempted to pick apart those around me.

I'm angry and offended... so I decide to hold a grudge and not forgive.

I feel overwhelmed and tired... so I begin to grow resentful and easily agitated.

I'm suffering through trials... so I begin to doubt God's faithfulness.

Do you notice a trend? All of these temptations are subtle, almost unrecognizable as temptations. And they are easily justifiable. (I'm entitled to feel this way - right?) Every one of these temptations deals with our feelings and emotions. The enemy plays to our weaknesses; and while emotions like sadness, anger, and frustration are normal, the enemy often sees them as open doors. He plays to our feelings of lack. Maybe we are experiencing a lack peace, joy, contentment, etc. And somehow, some way we will feel better if we take matters into our own hands.

So how do we deal with these temptations? The same way Jesus did. His feelings and emotions were justifiable in the wilderness. After all, it's only natural that the enemy would tempt Him with food while He was fasting for 40 days. But He didn't give in. And rather than simply say no, He chose to declare the truth. He turned his temptations into an opportunity to build spiritual strength.

When we declare the truth, the enemy's lies lose their power.

Here's the truth: <u>You lack nothing in Jesus.</u> Don't allow the enemy to lie to you and convince you that he has something you need. It is God who sustains you and meets your needs. You have the mind of Christ. With God on your side, there is nothing to fear. And you can say no to every temptation by the power of the Holy Spirit.

Both trials and temptations give us a chance to grow. Every time we say 'no' to temptation, we grow stronger in our ability to do so. And the more we declare truth when the enemy tries to lie to us and deceive us, the better we are at recognizing His lies in the first place. Trials help us to grow as well, but they are much different from temptations. Trials must be endured, and unlike temptations, God doesn't always provide a "way out."

I've heard it said that God doesn't give us more than we can handle. But unfortunately, there's no real biblical basis for this statement. It stems from 1 Corinthians 10:13 which tells us how God is faithful to not let us be tempted beyond our ability. But the key here is that this verse is talking about temptations, not trials. If we look throughout Scripture, we will find countless examples of those who faced trials that they couldn't handle on their own. The early Christians, for example, were heavily persecuted, even to the point of death.

God will often allow trials in our lives to show us our need for Him. In this way, we can <u>expect</u> to encounter trials that we can't handle apart from Him.

- **Trials produce spiritual growth. (Romans 5:3-5)**

- **Trials grant us the opportunity to experience true joy and peace from the Lord that is beyond our understanding. (James 1:2-4)**

- **Perseverance through difficult times always brings great reward and spiritual blessing. (1 Peter 4:12-13, James 1:12)**

Trials come in all shapes and sizes. Maybe you're dealing with the loss of a loved one. Or perhaps a chronic illness is weighing you down. Or if you're like me, simple day-to-day stress tries to steal my joy. In every trial, God is faithful to help us endure. He comforts and strengthens us as we grow in our faith.

Trials will come. The Bible says so. But the Bible also tells us that we can choose joy in the midst of these trials. We can view them through the lens of eternity, and we will always be victorious because Christ has already overcome the world.

Week 7 Study Guide:

- What weapons do we have as believers to fight off the enemy's lies?

- According to 2 Corinthians 10:3-5, what power do our God-given weapons hold and how does this comfort you for the fight?

- In your own words, define what it means to take every thought prisoner making them obey the Messiah?

- Can you think of a time when you made the conscious choice to take a thought captive? What was the result?

- According to James 1:13-15, what's the result of a sinful desire that we have allowed to "conceive"?

- What truth do we learn about Jesus and temptation in Hebrews 2:17-18? How does this comfort you?

- According to Romans 5:3-5, what is the final result of enduring through our struggles?

- What additional results do we find in James 1:2-4, 12?

Week 8: The Mind of Christ

HIS STRENGTH IN OUR WEAKNESS

"Little ones to Him belong; they are weak, but He is strong." I remember learning these words to *Jesus Loves Me* as a child. (I can still remember the arm motions.) From an early age, I learned that even in my weakness, He is strong - a concept that I'm still working on putting into practice today.

But I have learned one crucial detail in my adult years that goes beyond what I learned as a child. I may be weak, but God doesn't intend on me living my life as a weak person. I can't keep walking around declaring how weak I am; rather, I need to learn to be strong in Him.

God longs to take our weakness and exchange it for His strength.

...for this reason, to keep me from exalting myself, there was given me a thorn in the flesh, a messenger of Satan to torment me—to keep me from exalting myself! Concerning this I implored the Lord three times that it might leave me. And He has said to me, "My grace is sufficient for you, for power is perfected in weakness." Most gladly, therefore, I will rather boast about my weaknesses, so that the power of Christ may dwell in me. Therefore I am well content with weaknesses, with insults, with distresses, with persecutions, with difficulties, for Christ's sake; for when I am weak, then I am strong. - 2 Corinthians 12:7-10

This particular passage in 2 Corinthians has long been debated by scholars and Bible teachers. What exactly was Paul talking about when he mentions having a thorn in his flesh? Some say it was an illness, but I believe the verse says it all.

1. *Paul refers to the thorn as a "messenger of Satan."*
2. *In verse 10, he gives us a list of his weaknesses: insults, hardships, persecutions, and difficulties.*

So basically, his thorn could have been anything and everything he was encountering in his ministry. And two things are certain: the thorn was from the enemy and God chose to leave the thorn alone (for now) to keep Paul from becoming proud. But God doesn't leave Paul empty-handed. He reminds him of His perfect grace and that good things would come from his current circumstances.

God supplied grace and strength to Paul throughout his difficulties, but Paul *grew in strength* when he chose to be "content" in his weaknesses. In other words, when he chose to rejoice in his sufferings rather than wallow in them, he grew stronger.

God does supply a measure of strength in our lives, but we have to learn to rely on His strength in order for it to grow.

Paul understood what it meant to rely on God's strength:

We rely on His strength when we choose to see our trials through His eyes instead of our own.

We rely on His strength when we trust that His plans will exceed our expectations and that He will work everything together for our good.

And we rely on His strength when we choose joy in the midst of difficult circumstances.

The secret to being content is to always rely on God's strength - to make the daily choice to be strong in Him.

THE MIND OF CHRIST: UNITED IN THOUGHT AND PURPOSE

Are we united as Christians? It's a simple question. Yes or no. But the truth is that it's not necessarily that simple. Okay... maybe it is, and we just don't like the answer. For one thing, a quick Google search reveals that we have over 34,000+ denominations. (My jaw actually dropped when I read this!) I understand the need to attend a church that views certain particulars of Scripture the way you do, but is this what Jesus wanted when He prayed in the garden that we would be united as believers? (John 17:20-23) Is this what Paul meant when he reminded us that we have the mind of Christ and that we should be united by this fact?

If I'm being honest, it's not the number of denominations that bothers me. It's the way we treat each other.

Let me give you some background. I live in a smaller town with quite a few churches. I have witnessed first-hand people shunning one another because they attend a different church. And not just once, but on numerous occasions. I've heard the gossip that circulates when someone leaves one church for another, and I've seen this both in terms of the congregation as well as the leadership. Aren't we all part of one body? One faith? And one Spirit?

56

There's no doubt that our Christian walk was meant to be shared with one another. We are all in this together. Yet over time, the enemy has used our disagreements over theology and doctrine to segregate and divide us. And I'm not saying that it is wrong necessarily that we have denominations of like-minded believers. I am, however, acknowledging how we treat one another based on these differences.

Paul addressed the same issue in his letter to the Romans. They were fighting over what foods were acceptable to eat and which days they should worship. They were letting these small disputes get in the way of what really mattered - their faith in Jesus.

For the kingdom of God is not eating and drinking, but righteousness and peace and joy in the Holy Spirit. For he who in this way serves Christ is acceptable to God and approved by men. So then we pursue the things which make for peace and the building up of one another. Do not tear down the work of God for the sake of food. All things indeed are clean, but they are evil for the man who eats and gives offense. - Romans 14:17-20

Anyone who bows the knee to Jesus, who receives the truth of the gospel and becomes a child of God, is your brother and sister in Christ. It doesn't matter what church they go to or where they stand on minor theological issues. As Paul said, "Don't tear apart the word of God" over something that has no effect on your salvation.

We are all part of the same family. And we are called to be of one mind - and that is the mind of Christ.

CREATED FOR LOVE: DESIGNED IN THE IMAGE OF OUR LOVING FATHER

Did you know you were created for love? In the beginning, God made man in His image. All was perfect. The garden was perfect, man was perfect, and God's relationship with man was perfect. But then the enemy stepped in and deceived them into thinking that God was hiding something from them. He caused them to question God and His character, and in doing so, he managed to tempt Eve to take a bite from the forbidden tree. The consequences of that decision were severe, to say the least.

The one who does not love does not know God, for God is love. - 1 John 4:8

If God is love and we were made in His image, then we were made in the image of love.

God created us in love. And even when we rebelled and lived in sin, He still loved us. In His love, He sent Jesus so that once again we could be made perfect in His love.

From the beginning, it's been all about love. Why? Because God is love. It's who He is. And therefore, it's how He created us to be as well.

If we are children of God, that makes us children of love. Think about it this way:

Who created us? Love

Why did He create us? Love

What did Jesus call the greatest commandment? Love.

Why did He die for our sins? Love.

How are we called to live as believers? Love.

You were designed by love, in His image, making you created for love.

So what does this mean for us and our renewed minds? Well... everything. A renewed mind in Christ is one that lives in a constant state of love. We love God with all we have, and we love others the way Jesus loved us.

If I'm being honest, it's a lot easier for me to love God than it is to love others. I hate admitting that, but it's true. God is faithful and true, and I long to show Him love and adoration. But others... it's hard to love others sometimes. Loving others means that I love everyone, even those who hurt and offend me or those who simply "rub me the wrong way" and get on my nerves. It means forgiving unconditionally... even without an apology.

Jesus laid down His life for us even when we were still in our sin. This is how we are called to love others.

But there's good news for people like me. God is love. And when I surrendered my life to Him, I was given the mind of Christ. I don't have to rely on my own ability to show love; rather the Holy Spirit transforms my mind to love the way God loves.

I was created for love. And now that God's love dwells within me, I can be who He created me to be.

We have come to know and have believed the love which God has for us. God is love, and the one who abides in love abides in God, and God abides in him. - 1 John 4:16

IF YOU'RE GOING TO SPEAK YOUR MIND, MAKE SURE IT'S RENEWED

So here we are at the end of our journey. Throughout the process of writing for this study, I've had my fair share of ups and downs. In all my research and planning, I found myself being challenged by the things God was laying on my heart to share. Having a renewed mind isn't just a suggestion found in the Bible, it's the very foundation of Christian living. *You can't truly live for God without surrendering your mind to Him.*

Renewing your mind is more than surrender, however. It requires action on our part. Yes, the Holy Spirit transforms us, and we have His power and guidance as we grow. But we are the ones who must make the effort to change our thinking. We have to be ready and willing to submit to the Holy Spirit, take every thought prisoner, and intentionally guard our minds against the schemes of the enemy. It's a daily process of learning how to walk in our new God-given identities. We have the mind of Christ, but it's up to us to use it.

Jesus changed the game when He addressed the Pharisees regarding the Law. They obeyed outwardly, but their minds and their hearts were far from God. While they thought of themselves as righteous and obedient, Jesus taught them that obedience begins within a person. They were far from righteous because their intentions were self-seeking.

Everything we do, good or bad, starts in the mind. The Bible describes this chain of events in the book of James:

Let no one say when he is tempted, "I am being tempted by God"; for God cannot be tempted by evil, and He Himself does not tempt anyone. But each one is tempted when he is carried away and enticed by his own lust. Then when lust has conceived, it gives birth to sin; and when sin is accomplished, it brings forth death. - James 1:13-15

Temptation isn't limited to outward sins. Personally speaking, I'm often tempted by worry, doubts, and fear. But every temptation, regardless of the sin, begins the same way - in the mind. It's a desire, something that entices us, or something that we think will make us feel better. But notice how this verse says that temptation gives birth to sin *after* it has been conceived. Temptations will come, but if we allow them to "conceive," that's when we have a problem.

We uproot negative thinking and temptation when we daily make the choice to live with renewed minds by the power of the Holy Spirit.

Our perspective, our intentions, our feelings, and our emotions... they all shape our behavior. And all of these things can be changed if we're willing to put forth the effort. I can CHOOSE to see my husband differently. I can CHOOSE to not be offended or resentful of others. And I can CHOOSE to focus on the unseen rather than the seen. *Daily making these choices is a part of renewing your mind.*

The other part of having a renewed mind involves the Holy Spirit. Think about the fruit of the Spirit for a moment: love, joy, peace, patience, kindness, goodness, faithfulness, gentleness, and self-control. When we allow the Spirit to take control and daily submit to His will, we can *expect* to produce this fruit in our lives.

And I'm not just talking about outward actions. In fact, most of the Holy Spirit's "fruit" happens within our minds. They are feelings and emotions that affect our outward actions. *Our actions begin to stem from godly thinking and our thinking begins to match our godly living.* Every word we speak and every deed we accomplish is birthed from a renewed mind that has been completely transformed.

We can rest assured that when the Holy Spirit transforms us by the renewing of our minds, it's a complete transformation - inside and out.

Week 8 Study Guide:

- According to Philippians 4:12-13, what is the result of relying on God's strength in every situation?

- What challenge did Paul give us as Christians in 1 Corinthians 1:10? What do you think hinders us from fulfilling this challenge?

- Read Romans 15:5-6. What can we rely on as we strive to be united as believers?

- According to Philippians 2:1-5, what are some of the keys to living in harmony as the body of Christ?

- Read 1 John 4:9-12. How did God demonstrate His love for us? What should be our response?

- In your own words, describe what it means to be created in love and for love.

- When it comes to loving others, what does it mean to see those around us through the eyes of Christ? What are some practical ways we can put this into practice?

- Based on what you've learned throughout this study, what steps do you plan on taking to ensure that you are living with the mind of Christ in all that you do?

ABOUT THE AUTHOR

Alyssa J Howard is a wife and stay-at-home mom to two young girls. She lives with her family in the Pacific Northwest where she loves to bake, run, drink coffee, and dance with her daughters. Alyssa first fell in love with writing while earning her Master of Arts degree in theological studies through Liberty Theological Seminary. And while she's not writing Bible studies, you can find her writing about Jesus and the Christian life at alyssajhoward.com. She is also proud to be a part of the Hello Mornings writing team (hellomornings.org) as well as the writing team for Do Not Depart (donotdepart.com).

Made in the USA
Las Vegas, NV
05 March 2021

19054035R00039